Ken's Story Part 2

I Talk You Talk Press

CONTENTS

I Talk You Talk Press

IMPORTANT!

This book is Part 2 of Ken's Story. The story starts in *Ken's Story Part 1*.

This story is set in Japan. In the story, there are some Japanese words.

The Japanese words are

1. *san* - Mr/Ms (E.g. Tanaka san = Mr Tanaka)
2. *kanpai* - Cheers!
3. *Yonago* - a city in Japan
4. *Izumo Taisha* - a famous shrine in Japan
5. *Mt. Daisen* - a mountain in West Japan
6. *bucho* - department manager

CHAPTER ONE

That evening, Ken and Saho go to a quiet bar and talk about the problem.

"I waited a long time to find a nice girlfriend," says Ken. "And, now that you are my girlfriend, I want to stay with you."

"I know. But I don't want a long-distance relationship," says Saho. "Yonago City is very far from here. I don't want a boyfriend in Yonago. I want a boyfriend here, in Tokyo."

"But I like you very much Saho. Let's stay together. I will come back to Tokyo every month to see you. I promise," says Ken.

"Ken, that's too hard for you. If you come back to Tokyo every month, you will be very tired," says Saho.

"It's OK. I want to see you. I will be tired, but I will also be happy. Please Saho!" says Ken.

Saho drinks her wine and looks at Ken. He is very kind, and he likes her very much. She also likes him very much.

"OK, let's see how it goes," says Saho. "I will also visit you in Yonago."

"Yes! Thank you so much Saho!" says Ken.

Ken and Saho decide to stay together. Ken will come back to Tokyo once a month to see Saho, and Saho will also visit Ken in Yonago.

It is Sunday morning. Ken and Saho are at Haneda Airport. Ken checks in.

"Goodbye Ken. Have a good flight. Send me an email when you

arrive at Yonago Airport," says Saho.

"Yes, I will. Goodbye Saho," says Ken.

Ken gets on the airplane. Saho watches the airplane fly up into the sky. She watches until it disappears into the clouds. Then, she takes the train back into the centre of Tokyo, and she goes home alone.

An hour later, Ken sends Saho an email.

---*I arrived in Yonago! I'll email you later tonight!*---

Saho replies:

---*I'm glad you arrived safely. Good luck!*---

She is pleased that Ken arrived safely in Yonago. She tries to watch TV, but she cannot stop thinking about Ken. It is a very sad day for Saho.

Ken arrives at his company apartment in Yonago. He looks around the apartment. It is very small. There is one room, a small kitchen, a toilet and a very small bathroom. He opens the window and walks out onto the balcony. The apartment is opposite a rice field. The rice field is very green and there is a very nice breeze. It is very peaceful and very quiet. It is very different from Ken's apartment in Tokyo. In Tokyo, his apartment was next to a railway line. He could hear trains all day and all night. Here, in his apartment in Yonago, he can only hear the birds singing.

Ken feels very tired. He falls asleep listening to the gentle wind and the birds singing.

Ken wakes up. He looks at his mobile phone. It is 3:30am. There is a message from Saho.

---*Are you OK? I waited for your email. Please email me when you have time. From Saho.*---

Oh no! I fell asleep! I didn't email Saho! thinks Ken. *It's too late now. Saho will be sleeping. I'll email her in the morning.*

Ken goes back to sleep.

CHAPTER TWO

Ken wakes up at 7:00am. He is very nervous because today is his first day at the office in Yonago.

I hope my new boss is nice, he thinks. *I hope my co-workers are kind.*

He is too nervous to eat breakfast. He brushes his teeth and irons his shirt. He gets dressed and watches the local news on TV. He looks out of the window. It is raining. He has no umbrella. He decides to buy an umbrella on the way to the bus stop. He puts on his shoes and walks outside. He locks his apartment door and goes to the convenience store near his apartment. He buys an umbrella and a can of coffee.

He gets the bus to his office. His office is in the centre of Yonago City. He goes into the office. His boss greets him and introduces him to his new co-workers. Eight people work in the office. It is a lot smaller than the Tokyo office.

Ken works until 12:00pm. Then, he goes to a convenience store to buy a lunch box. He looks at his mobile phone.

Oh no! I forgot to email Saho again! he thinks.

He emails Saho.

---*Saho, I'm very sorry. I forgot about you because I was very busy!*---

Saho replies:

---*You forgot about me?*---

Oh no, thinks Ken. *That was a bad thing to write. Saho is angry.*

He writes:

---*I'm sorry Saho. I will call you tonight when I finish work. I promise.*---

Saho replies:

---OK, I will wait for your call.---

In the afternoon, Ken has a meeting.

"Good afternoon everyone," says Ken's boss. "Ken Maeda, from Tokyo, has joined our office. So we are going to have a welcome party tonight. We are going to go to a restaurant near the station."

Everyone smiles at Ken.

Ken smiles at everyone. He is looking forward to drinking with his new co-workers.

That evening, everyone finishes work at 5:30pm. They go to the restaurant. They sit around a table and order some beer. Ken makes a speech.

"Good evening everyone. I am very happy to transfer to Yonago and to work with you in the Yonago office. I look forward to working with you all, and I will do my best. Thank you."

Everyone claps. "Cheers!" "Kanpai!" "Cheers!" They all drink beer. It is very delicious.

Ken has a nice time with his co-workers. They talk about many things. They talk about Yonago, Tottori and Tokyo. A co-worker, Saki Fujimoto, is sitting next to him. She is nineteen and very cute.

"Maeda san, do you know Izumo Taisha shrine?" asks Saki.

"Yes, I do, but I have never been there," says Ken.

"It's a very nice place. It's not so far from Yonago. Many people go to the shrine to pray for help in finding a marriage partner," says Saki. "I hope I can meet a nice man, so I go to Izumo Taisha a lot. We can go together sometime," she says.

"Yes, that would be very nice! Thank you Fujimoto san," says Ken. He is very happy.

"Call me Saki! Everyone in the office calls me Saki," says Saki.

"OK, I will. And you can call me Ken. All my friends and co-workers in Tokyo call me Ken," says Ken.

"OK, I will!" says Saki.

By the end of the party, everybody is drunk. One of Ken's co-workers has a camera.

"Let's take a photograph!" he says.

They take a photograph. Everybody is smiling and is very happy. Ken gets home at 10:30pm. He is very drunk and very tired. He looks at his mobile phone. There is a missed call from Saho.

Oh no! Saho! I forgot again! he thinks. *I must call her now! She will be very angry!*

He calls Saho.

"Hello," says Saho.

"Hello! Saki! I'm so sorry! I forgot! I went to a restaurant with my co-workers and I had a few beers and…" says Ken.

"Ken, who is Saki?" says Saho.

"Saki? What? How do you know about Saki?" asks Ken.

"You called me Saki. You said 'Hello! Saki! I'm so sorry! I forgot!'" says Saho. "So…who is Saki?"

"Oh, I'm sorry. I made a mistake Saho. Saki Fujimoto is my new co-worker. We were talking at the restaurant for a long time," says Ken.

"Oh, I see," says Saho. "Did you have a nice time?"

"Yes! It was wonderful! I had a great time! Everyone is very friendly and Yonago is a very nice place!"

"Oh good. I'm glad you are having a nice time," says Saho. She feels a little upset. Ken forgot about her. And he called her Saki.

Later, Saho looks at Facebook. She sees a photograph of Ken and his co-workers in the restaurant. The woman sitting next to him is young and beautiful. Saho looks at the name. Saki Fujimoto.

So, that is Saki, thinks Saho sadly.

CHAPTER THREE

One Saturday, a month later, Saho calls Ken.

"Hello," says Ken.

"Hi Ken. It's Saho!" says Saho.

"Hi Saho! How are you?" asks Ken.

"I'm good thanks. Where are you?" asks Saho.

"I'm at Izumo Taisha! It is a beautiful shrine! There are many people here," says Ken. "Many people pray here when they want to find love."

"Are you at Izumo Taisha alone?" asks Saho.

"No, I'm not. I'm here with Saki," says Ken.

"With Saki?" says Saho.

"Yes, Saki is giving me a tour of Izumo today. Later, we are going to a lighthouse called Hinomisaki, and then we are going to the Izumo History Museum," says Ken.

"Oh, I see. Well, have a nice time," says Saho sadly. "Ken, when will you come back to Tokyo? Will you come back next weekend?"

"Next weekend? No, I can't come back next weekend," says Ken.

"Why not? Are you too busy?" asks Saho.

"Yes, I'm very busy. I'm going to the Oki Islands," says Ken.

"The Oki Islands? Where are the Oki Islands?" asks Saho.

"The Oki Islands are small islands in the Sea of Japan. They are very beautiful. They have very nice beaches and they are very quiet and peaceful," says Ken.

"Oh, I see. Are you going alone?" asks Saho.

"No, I'm not. I'm going with Saki. We are working on the same

7

project, so we have to go together," says Ken.

"Oh… I see. Well…good luck," says Saho.

"Yes, thanks! You too! Bye!" says Ken.

"Bye!" says Saho.

Saho feels very upset. Of course, she is happy because Ken is enjoying his new life in Yonago. But, she is sad because Ken has no time to see her. He doesn't email or call her very often. Before he went to Yonago, he promised to come back to Tokyo once a month. But, he hasn't come back to Tokyo yet. And Saki…he is always with Saki.

Maybe I should forget about Ken. He has no time for me now. He has a new life, new friends…and maybe a new girlfriend, thinks Saho.

She spends all weekend thinking about her future.

Two weeks later, Saho is looking at Facebook. She sees a photograph. In the photograph, Ken and Saki are standing in front of the sea and a sunset in the Oki Islands. It looks very romantic. They are smiling and they look very happy. Also, they are standing very close to each other. Saho looks at the photograph caption.

It says: *Ken and I in the Oki Islands! Ken is my cool, handsome friend from Tokyo!*

"Ken is my cool, handsome friend from Tokyo!" Saho reads the comment again.

"What? That is my boyfriend!" she says. She looks at the other comments on the photograph.

The first comment is from Ken.

Saki! Thank you! It is a very nice picture! You look very cute!

"You look cute? You look cute? I don't believe this!" says Saho, angrily. "That's it! Finished! I never want to see Ken again!"

CHAPTER FOUR

It is Monday morning.

"Good morning Saho," says Yumiko.

"Good morning Yumiko," says Saho.

"Saho, what's wrong? You don't look happy. Are you OK?" asks Yumiko.

"No, I am not OK," says Saho.

Saho tells Yumiko about Ken and Saki. She shows Yumiko the photograph and the comments on Facebook. She tells Yumiko about Ken going to Izumo Taisha with Saki.

"I will talk to Ken about it," says Yumiko.

"No, it's OK. Forget it. I'm going to forget about him. I'm going to find a new boyfriend in Tokyo," says Saho.

"No, Saho. Please wait. Ken likes you. But he doesn't understand women. You know that. He doesn't know that you are sad and angry. I think Ken and Saki are just friends. He likes you, not Saki," says Yumiko.

"Really? I don't think so," says Saho. "He never calls me. He forgets to email me. And, he is always with Saki. They are always together."

Yumiko looks at Saho. She feels sorry for Saho, and she really wants to help her.

"Saho, I have an idea," says Yumiko.

"What?" asks Saho.

"Are you busy next weekend?" asks Yumiko.

"No, I don't have any plans. Why?"

"You should go to Yonago next weekend! You can meet Ken and talk to him. Tell him that you are not happy. Tell him that you are worried about him and Saki. You can enjoy sightseeing, and spending time together."

"I don't know, Yumiko. Maybe I should forget about Ken," says Saho.

"Do you still like him?" asks Yumiko.

Saho thinks for a minute.

"Yes, I do. I still like him very much," says Saho.

"So go to Yonago and see him!" says Yumiko.

"OK…yes…I think I will," says Saho. "I will go to Yonago!"

Saho calls Ken.

"Ken, can I come to Yonago next weekend?" asks Saho.

"Yes! Of course you can! We will have a very good time together! I really want to see you!" says Ken. "And there is a jazz festival on Saturday afternoon. We can go there together! I'll buy the tickets!"

Ken is excited because Saho will come to Yonago. He starts to plan their schedule. He wants to take her sightseeing near his new home.

CHAPTER FIVE

Saho arrives in Yonago on Saturday morning. The airport is a lot smaller and quieter than Haneda Airport in Tokyo. She stands outside the airport and waits for Ken. It is very sunny, and the air is very clear.

This is a nice place, thinks Saho. *I'm looking forward to spending time here with Ken.*

"Saho! Saho!"

Saho looks up and sees Ken running towards her.

"Sorry I'm late! There was a lot of traffic on the roads," says Ken. "How are you?"

"I'm good, thanks," says Saho. She smiles at him shyly. "It is good to see you Ken."

"And it's great to see you too, Saho. We are going to have a great time! Oh, let me carry your bag!" says Ken.

Saho is surprised. "Oh thank you! Your dating manners are excellent Ken!"

"I had a good teacher!" says Ken. They both laugh.

Ken takes Saho to a noodle restaurant for lunch. Then, they go to the jazz festival. After that, they go to Mt Daisen, a mountain near Yonago.

"This is a beautiful place Ken. We can see the sea, and the air is so fresh and clear," says Saho. "It's good to get away from Tokyo for a few days. I feel so happy and relaxed."

"Good! I'm glad you feel that way. I feel happy and relaxed too!"

says Ken.

"What shall we do tonight?" asks Saho. "Shall we go out for dinner?"

"Tonight? I already made plans," says Ken. "I told my boss and co-workers about your trip to Yonago. They want to meet you."

"Really? Did you tell them that we are dating? Did you tell them that I am your girlfriend?" asks Saho.

"No, of course not! That is a secret! I told them you were my co-worker from Tokyo! I told them you like jazz, so you wanted to visit the jazz festival," says Ken.

"Why didn't you tell them that I am your girlfriend?" asks Saho.

"Because we work in the same company. We should keep our romance a secret," says Ken.

"Oh, I see," says Saho. "So your co-workers think you don't have a girlfriend?"

"That's right! My co-worker Saki asked me 'Do you have a girlfriend?' and I said 'No, I don't have a girlfriend'. So it is a secret!" says Ken.

"Will Saki come out tonight?" asks Saho.

"Yes, she will! She is looking forward to meeting you," says Ken.

Ken told his co-workers he doesn't have a girlfriend. Saho feels a little sad, but she understands the reason. The company doesn't like office romances.

That evening, they go to a yakitori restaurant with Ken's co-workers. Saho is sitting next to Ken's boss and Ken is sitting next to Saki. Ken and Saki talk to each other all night. They look very happy. Saho talks to Ken's boss. Everyone is very nice, but she doesn't have a good time. Ken doesn't talk to her. He only talks to Saki.

Ken doesn't like me anymore. He only likes Saki, she thinks. She goes to the toilets and looks at her face in the mirror. Her face looks so sad. She puts some lipstick on. Then, the door opens and Saki walks in.

"Oh hi! It's very nice to meet you!" says Saki.

"Yes, it is very nice to meet you, too," says Saho. "Do you enjoy working in the office?"

"Well, before, I didn't like my job, but now I really like it," says Saki.

"Really? Why? What changed?" asks Saho.

"Ken came from Tokyo! He is a very nice man and we have a great time together! We talk all the time! We always laugh together and go out together at weekends!" says Saki. "I think he likes me!"

"Oh really? That's nice," says Saho quietly. She goes into the toilet and locks the door. She emails Yumiko.

---I am going to finish with Ken. He has a new girlfriend now.---

Ken and Saho are at Yonago Airport. They are waiting for Saho's flight back to Tokyo. They have some time before Saho's flight, so they are having coffee in a café.

"Saho, are you OK? You are very quiet," says Ken. He is worried. Saho has been very quiet since last night.

"Yes, I'm fine," says Saho.

"When can I see you again?" asks Ken.

"You can see me at the general meeting in Tokyo next month," says Saho.

"Will you come to Yonago again Saho?" asks Ken.

Saho looks at Ken. Then, she looks at the table. She shakes her head. "I don't think so Ken," says Saho.

"Why not?" asks Ken.

"Ken, you have a new girlfriend now. Forget about me," says Saho.

"What? New girlfriend? Who? I don't understand!" says Ken. He is very shocked.

"I think you understand Ken. Forget it. I don't want to see you again." Saho stands up. "Oh, look at the time! My flight leaves soon! Goodbye Ken. I hope you and Saki are very happy together."

Saho stands up, picks up her bag and goes to the gate.

"Saki? What? Saho! Wait! I don't understand! What are you talking about?" Ken stands up. *Saki? New girlfriend? What is Saho talking about?* he thinks. *I really don't understand women at all...*

CHAPTER SIX

It is Monday morning. Saho and Yumiko are drinking coffee at work. Saho is telling Yumiko about her trip to Yonago.

"Saki and Ken are always together. They go to many places together," says Saho. "And Saki likes him very much. She told me. Ken has no time for me now. He likes Saki."

"I don't think so," says Yumiko. "Ken doesn't understand women very well. Did you talk to him about Saki?"

"No, I didn't. I wanted to, but after I spoke to Saki, I was very unhappy. I decided to forget about Ken. I will look for a new boyfriend in Tokyo," says Saho.

"But, do you still like Ken?" asks Yumiko.

"Yes, I do. I like him a lot," says Saho quietly. Then, she stands up and says very strongly, "but I don't want to see him. It's over! It's finished!"

Yumiko decides to call Ken.

"Hello, Maeda speaking," says Ken.

"Ken, it's Yumiko," says Yumiko.

"Yumiko, hello!" says Ken.

"How was your weekend with Saho?" asks Yumiko.

"Well, it is strange. I had a good time, but Saho was not happy. She doesn't want to see me anymore! She thinks I have a new girlfriend! But I don't have a new girlfriend! I only like Saho! I don't understand!" says Ken.

"Why does Saho think you have a new girlfriend?" asks Yumiko.

"I don't know," says Ken. "It's very strange."

"No, Ken! It is not strange! You and Saki are spending a lot of time together," says Yumiko.

"Yes, we are. She is my friend," says Ken.

"Ken, I have seen the photographs of you and Saki on Facebook. You look like a couple! Of course Saho is upset!" says Yumiko.

"Saki and I are not a couple! We are just friends!" says Ken.

"I know! But in the photographs you look like a couple! And you are always talking about Saki. And, you didn't tell your co-workers about you and Saho! You said 'It is a secret!' I understand the reason. I know that our company doesn't like office romances, but, of course Saho is not happy," says Yumiko.

"Oh, I see. What can I do?" asks Ken.

"I don't know, Ken. Saho doesn't want to see you anymore," says Yumiko.

"But I really like Saho! I really like her! Oh no! I feel very bad. I did a bad thing…" says Ken.

"No, you didn't do a very bad thing. Ken you don't understand women, or women's feelings! That's all! You have to think about Saho's feelings too!" says Yumiko.

"What should I do? Is it too late?" asks Ken.

"You have to talk to her! Tell her your true feelings!" says Yumiko.

"OK, I will email her tonight," says Ken.

"No Ken! Not by email!" says Yumiko.

"OK, I will call her," says Ken.

"No! You have to come to Tokyo!" says Yumiko. "Talk to her directly!"

"When?" asks Ken.

"This weekend! Do you have any plans?" asks Yumiko.

"Yes, I do. Saki and I are going for a drive. We are going to Mt. Daisen," says Ken.

"Ken! Is Saki your girlfriend? Tell me the truth!" Yumiko is angry now.

"No, she isn't. Saho is…or was…my girlfriend," says Ken.

"Who is more important to you, Saki or Saho?" asks Yumiko.

"Saho of course," says Ken. "Of course Saho is more important!"

"Then cancel your date with Saki and come to Tokyo to see Saho!" says Yumiko.

"It is not a date with Saki! We are going for a drive, that's all. It is

15

not a date!" says Ken.

"Ken, you must cancel it! Cancel it and come to Tokyo!" says Yumiko. She is very angry.

"OK, I will. I'll come to Tokyo. I promise," says Ken.

CHAPTER SEVEN

Saho and Ken are sitting in a coffee shop in Roppongi in Tokyo. Saho looks out of the window. It is raining. Many people are walking along the street. Saho sees a couple walking together under an umbrella. *They look happy,* she thinks.

"Saho, I promise. I'm not interested in Saki. We are just friends. I only like you," says Ken.

"It's not only that. You live in Yonago. I live in Tokyo. You are very busy every day. You have no time to call me or email me. Long distance relationships are difficult," says Saho.

"I can change!" says Ken.

"How?" asks Saho. "You say 'I can change', but I don't think you can change."

"I will call you and email you every day! I will come back to Tokyo every weekend!" says Ken.

"You said that before. You promised me. But you didn't come back to Tokyo," says Saho.

"This time is different. I promise! When I moved to Yonago, I had no friends. I was lonely. I wanted to make new friends. I wanted to go sightseeing in Yonago. I wanted to spend time with my new co-workers. If we spend time together and become friends, we will work better together. Now, I usually spend my weekends with Saki, but I will change! I will come back to Tokyo and spend every weekend with you!" says Ken.

"Every weekend?" asks Saho.

"Yes. Saho, you are very important to me. You are my girlfriend," says Ken. "I promise. I will come back every weekend."

"Really? Do you promise?" asks Saho.

"Yes, I do! I promise!" says Ken.

Saho looks at Ken. He looks so honest. And Saho knows that Ken is a good man. They have been friends and co-workers for many years.

He is a good man, really, thinks Saho. She smiles at him.

"OK, let's try," says Saho.

"Thank you Saho! I promise I will be a good boyfriend!" says Ken. "I promise!"

In the evening, Saho emails Yumiko.

---Ken and I are going to try again. He promised to come back to Tokyo every weekend to see me.---

Yumiko replies:

---That's great news! I'm very happy for you both!---

CHAPTER EIGHT

Ken goes back to Tokyo every weekend to see Saho. It is very expensive and he is very tired every week. Sometimes, on Monday mornings, he is late for work. Sometimes, he falls asleep at his desk. His boss is not happy.

"Maeda san, why are you always so tired?" asks his boss. "What do you do at the weekend?"

"I usually go back to Tokyo," says Ken.

"Every weekend?" asks his boss.

"Yes, every weekend," says Ken.

"Why?" asks his boss.

"To see my family and friends," says Ken.

"To see your girlfriend?" asks his boss. "Do you have a girlfriend in Tokyo?"

"Er…yes," says Ken quietly.

"Going to Tokyo to see your girlfriend is fine. But, falling asleep and being late for work on Monday mornings is not fine. Do you understand?" says his boss.

"Yes, I do. I'm very sorry," says Ken.

"Next week, you will go to Korea on business, so you can't go to Tokyo next weekend," says his boss.

"Next week? Korea? Really?" says Ken. He is very surprised. "How long will I stay?"

"You will stay for five days," says his boss. "You will leave Japan on Friday night and come back on Wednesday. Saki will go with you."

19

Ken looks at the calendar. Friday…the 16th…Oh no! Saho's birthday is the 17th!

He calls Saho.

"Saho, I'm very sorry, but I can't come back to Tokyo next weekend," says Ken.

"Why not?" says Saho.

"Because I have to go to Korea on business," says Ken.

"Oh, I see. Well, it can't be helped," says Saho. "I'm disappointed, but work is important. I understand."

"I'm very sorry. It's your birthday on Saturday. I wanted to take you out for dinner. I wanted to take you to an expensive restaurant," says Ken.

"Don't worry, Ken. It's OK. We can go out the weekend after next," says Saho.

"Yes, let's do that," says Ken.

"Will you go to Korea alone?" asks Saho.

Ken thinks, *If I say 'I'm going to Korea with Saki', Saho will be angry…but I don't want to lie…What should I say?*

"I don't know. I think I am going to Korea alone," says Ken.

"Well, have a nice trip. I'll see you the week after next," says Saho.

"Yes, thank you. See you the week after next," says Ken.

CHAPTER NINE

It is Friday night. Saho is at home. She is looking at Facebook. She sees a photograph. She is very shocked. It is Ken and Saki. She reads the caption:

Ken and I are in Korea! We are having a great time!

"What? Oh my God! He lied to me!" shouts Saho angrily. "He isn't on a business trip! He is on vacation with Saki! He isn't alone! And it's my birthday tomorrow!"

She sends Ken a message on Facebook.

---I never want to see you again. Don't call me again. You liar!---

Ken is in a restaurant with Saki. He looks at the Facebook message on his smartphone. He starts to panic.

He thinks, *Oh no! Saki posted a photograph on Facebook! Saho saw it! She thinks I'm on vacation with Saki!*

He runs out of the restaurant and calls Saho. Saho does not answer her phone.

He sends her a message on Facebook.

---Saho, Saki and I are on a business trip together. I'm sorry, I didn't tell you. I didn't want to make you angry. So, I said, 'I think I am going to Korea alone'. I'm sorry. That was my mistake. Please forgive me.---

Then, Ken remembers. *Tomorrow is Saho's birthday! I haven't bought a birthday present for her yet! Oh no!* he thinks. He sits down on a wall and finds an Internet gift shop on his smartphone. He orders a very large bouquet of roses.

Today is Saturday. It is Saho's birthday, but she is not very happy. She does not want to celebrate. Many friends email and call her, but she does not reply. She stays in her apartment all day. At 4:00pm, the doorbell rings. She goes to the intercom. "Yes?"

"Saho Mochida, I have a delivery for you," says a man.

Saho opens the door. The delivery man is holding a large bouquet of red roses and a large cake. "These are for you," he says.

Saho is very surprised. "For me? Thank you," she says.

She takes the flowers and the cake and closes the door. There is also a card. She opens it and starts reading.

Dear Saho, These flowers and this cake are your birthday present. Please forgive me. I made a big mistake. I want to make you happy. I don't want to make you angry or sad. So, I didn't tell you the truth about my business trip. Saki and I work on the same project, so we had to go to Korea together. I wanted to spend your birthday with you. I am very shy, so it is difficult for me to say this. But…I love you. I love you a lot. When I come back to Japan, I will come to Tokyo to see you. From Ken

Saho starts to cry. The card is beautiful. Now, she understands Ken's feelings. She puts the flowers in three vases and eats the cake. It is strawberry and vanilla and it is very delicious. She eats it all. Then, she sends an email to Ken.

---Thank you for the flowers and cake. I read the card. I understand your feelings. I forgive you. Saho.---

Ken looks at the email from Saho. He is very happy. Saho forgives him.

But, I have to show Saho my feelings more, thinks Ken. *I really love Saho. What can I do?*

Ken thinks about it for a few days.

Then, when he goes back to Japan from Korea, he has a meeting with his boss at the Yonago office.

"I would like to transfer back to the Tokyo office," says Ken to his boss.

"Transfer back to the Tokyo office?" asks his boss. He is very surprised.

"Yes. Is it possible?" asks Ken.

"No, it isn't! You have to stay in Yonago for another year!" says his boss. "Don't you like Yonago?"

"Oh, I like Yonago very much…but…"

"It is only one more year! Work hard in Yonago for a year. Then, you can go back to Tokyo!" says his boss.

That night, Ken goes to a bar alone. He drinks whiskey and thinks about his life. While he is drinking, he makes a very big decision.

Two weeks later, Saho and Yumiko are at work. They are in a meeting.

"I have an announcement," says Fuji bucho. "The manager of the Yonago office called me. Ken Maeda has quit the company."

"What? He quit? Why?" says Yumiko.

"Really? Why?" says Saho.

Everyone is very shocked.

"I don't know the details, but the Yonago manager said Maeda san asked for a transfer back to the Tokyo office. Of course, that is not possible. So, the Yonago manager said 'No, Maeda san. You have to stay in Yonago for another year.' So, Maeda san quit," says Fuji bucho.

Saho goes to the toilet and calls Ken.

"Ken! Is it true? You quit?" asks Saho.

"Yes, it is," says Ken.

"Why?" asks Saho.

"Because I want to come back to Tokyo. I want to be near you," says Ken.

"But, Ken! It's your job! You liked your job! And you need money!" says Saho.

"It's OK. I found a new job in Tokyo. The salary is not so high, but the office is near your office!" says Ken. "We can see each other very often!"

Saho is very shocked.

"Where are you now Ken?" asks Saho.

"I am on the *shinkansen* bullet train. I will arrive in Tokyo at 6:00pm," says Ken. "What time do you finish work tonight?"

"5:30pm. I will come and meet you at Tokyo Station!" says Saho.

"Great! See you then!" says Ken.

"Ken?" says Saho.

"Yes?"

"Thank you," says Saho.

"You're welcome. Saho, I love you," says Ken.
Saho starts to cry. Now she understands. Ken loves her very much.
"Oh Ken! I love you too!" says Saho.
"We are going to be very happy together, Saho," says Ken.
Saho smiles. "Yes, we are!"

THANK YOU

Thank you for reading Ken's Story Part 2. (Word count: 5,566) We hope you enjoyed it.

There are quizzes about this book on our free study site I Talk You Talk Press EXTRA. http://italk-youtalk.com

If you would like to read more graded readers, please visit our website http://www.italkyoutalk.com

Other Level 1 graded readers include
A Business Trip to New York
A Homestay in Auckland
A Trip to London
Dear Ellen
Haruna's Story Part 1
Haruna's Story Part 2
Haruna's Story Part 3
Ken's Story Part 1
Life is Surprising!
Strange Stories
The Christmas Present
The Old Hospital
We Met Online

ABOUT THE AUTHOR

I Talk You Talk Press is a Japan-based publisher of language textbooks, graded readers and language learning/teaching resources.

Our team is made up of highly experienced language teachers and translators, who have all studied at least one additional language to an advanced level.

This experience enables us to design our materials from the perspective of both the teacher and the learner. We consult with both teachers and language learners when designing our textbooks and graded readers, and test our materials extensively in the classroom before publication.

We are a fast-growing press, and currently publish graded readers for learners of English. We publish new graded readers monthly.

www.ingramcontent.com/pod-product-compliance
Lightning Source LLC
Chambersburg PA
CBHW022351040426
42449CB00006B/828